11.95

P9-DFQ-006

# READING POWER

# Hulk Hogan
## Wrestling Pro
### Heather Feldman

The Rosen Publishing Group's
PowerKids Press ™
New York

For Sophie Megan

Published in 2001 by The Rosen Publishing Group, Inc.
29 East 21st Street, New York, NY 10010

First Edition

Book Design: Michael de Guzman

Photo Credits: pp. 5, 9, 11, 13, 15, 17, 21 © Colin Bowman; pp. 7, 19 © The Everett Collection.

Feldman, Heather.
    Hulk Hogan : wrestling pro / Heather Feldman.—1st ed.
        p. cm.— (Reading power)
    Includes index.
    Summary: A brief biography of the professional wrestler, focusing on his exploits in the ring, his career as a movie actor, and his charity work.
    ISBN 0-8239-5720-9 (alk. paper)
    1. Hogan, Hulk, 1955—Juvenile literature. 2. Wrestlers—United States—Biography—Juvenile literature. [1. Hogan, Hulk, 1955- 2. Wrestlers.] I. Title. II. Series.

GV1196.H64 F45 2001
796.812'092—dc21
[B]                                                          00-028006

Manufactured in the United States of America

2

# Contents

Hulk Hogan is a great wrestler. Hulk Hogan is very strong.

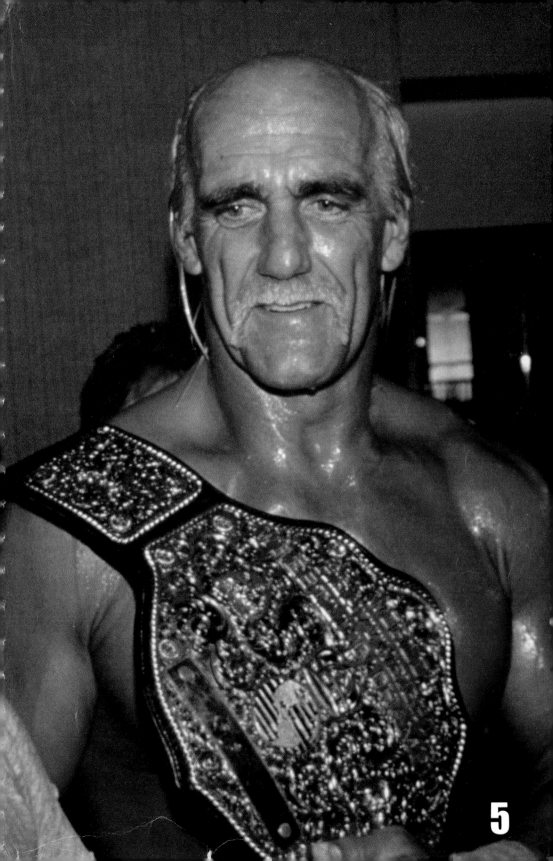

5

Hulk Hogan uses a weight machine. Hulk lifts weights to stay strong.

Hulk Hogan shows off his big muscles.

9

Hulk Hogan wrestles in a ring. Hulk Hogan has many fans. Lots of people like to watch him wrestle.

11

Hulk Hogan wins a belt for wrestling. Hulk Hogan is a wrestling pro.

13

Hulk Hogan talks to a reporter. Reporters ask Hulk questions because he is famous. Hulk meets a lot of people.

15

Hulk Hogan met
Muhammed Ali.

Hulk Hogan was in the movie *Rocky III*. Hulk played a mean wrestler named Thunderlips.

19

These children have bandannas like Hulk Hogan. These children like Hulk Hogan. Lots of people like Hulk Hogan!

# Glossary

**bandanna** (ban-DA-nah)  Colorful cloth worn on the head.

**belt** (BEHLT)  What a wrestler gets for winning a match.

**fans** (FANZ)  People who like a famous person.

**muscles** (MUH-suhlz)  Parts of the body underneath the skin that can be tightened or loosened to make the body move.

**reporter** (re-POR-ter)  a person who tells people the news.

**weights** (WAYTS)  Heavy objects that are lifted for exercise.

Here are more books to read
about wrestling:

*Wrestling Renegades: An In-Depth Look
at Today's Superstars of Pro Wrestling*
by Daniel Cohen
Archway (1999)

*Superstars of Men's Pro Wrestling*
by Matthew Hunter
Chelsea House Publishers (1998)

To learn more about Hulk Hogan,
check out these Web sites:

http://www.wrestlingmuseum.com/
   pages/bios/hogan2.html
http://www.wcwwrestling.com/1999
   /superstars/hogan/

# Index

Word Count: 129

## Note to Librarians, Teachers, and Parents

If reading is a challenge, Reading Power is a solution! Reading Power is perfect for readers who want high-interest subject matter at an accessible reading level. These fact-filled, photo-illustrated books are designed for readers who want straightforward vocabulary, engaging topics, and a manageable reading experience. With clear picture/text correspondence, leveled Reading Power books put the reader in charge. Now readers have the power to get the information they want and the skills they need in a user-friendly format.